Tap Tap Nap

Written by Clare Helen Welsh

Illustrated by Leesh Li

Collins

nap nap

tap tap

sit in

tap tap

nap nap

tap tap

pat pat

nap in it

tap tap

sit in it

nap nap

nap nap

After reading

> **Letters and Sounds:** Phase 2
>
> **Word count:** 26
>
> **Focus phonemes:** /s/ /a/ /t/ /p/ /i/ /n/
>
> **Curriculum links:** Personal, social and emotional development
>
> **Early learning goals:** Reading: use phonic knowledge to decode regular words and read them aloud accurately

Developing fluency

- Your child may enjoy hearing you read the book.
- Read the text together, having fun with the repeated words, **tap tap**. They could read **tap tap** on page 10 more loudly.

Phonic practice

- Point to and say the word **nap** on page 2. Ask your child if they can sound out each of the letter sounds, then blend them. (*n/a/p* – **nap**)
- Turn to page 8 and repeat for **pat**. (*p/a/t* – **pat**)
- Look at the "I spy sounds" pages (14 and 15). Point to and sound out the /p/ at the top of page 14, then point to the pineapple and say "pineapple", emphasising the /p/ sound. Point to the picture and say: It's a party – can you hear the /p/ sound in party? Take turns to name objects in the picture. Ask: Does that have the /p/ sound? Repeat the word if it does. (e.g. *parcel/present/packet, pineapple, pears, planet, popcorn, party popper, pizza*)

Extending vocabulary

- Turn to pages 8 and 9. Ask your child: Lots of of aliens are having a nap here. Can you think of another word that means the same as **nap**? (e.g. *sleep, doze*) Talk about how we know when someone is asleep or having a nap, encouraging vocabulary to do with sleep, e.g. dreams, closed eyes, bed, night, tired.